A Passion
for the Teaching
and Learning Process

Memories of Real Kids and Real Teachers in Real Schools

by Charyll Boggs

RoseDog Books
PITTSBURGH, PENNSYLVANIA 15238

RoseDog Books
585 Alpha Drive
Suite 103
Pittsburgh, PA 15238
Visit our website at *www.rosedogbookstore.com*

ISBN: 978-1-63867-408-5
eISBN: 978-1-63867-509-9

Dedication

I could not begin to name all the family, friends and colleagues who encouraged me through the process of writing this book. There were endless detours and roadblocks but they never let me give up. I view this work as my legacy, a history of my travels through many decades in the world of teaching and learning. I had the good fortune of meeting educators and students that taught me something new every day. That is a journey I have never and will never regret. It was an opportunity for me to pursue my dream of becoming a life-long learner and support that world of teaching and learning. It's what I wish for each and every student and teacher in a classroom today.

Table of Contents

Preface

As I was discussing my rough draft with a colleague whom I hold in the highest esteem, she commented that I appeared to put "Maslow before Bloom". What does that mean? One might recall that these are two notable authorities in the field of education.

There's a reason why the phrase Maslow before Bloom is so important. How a person develops through Maslow's hierarchy directly impacts their capacity and attention toward learning, both academic and social-emotional learning. (Mullen, 2020).

First let me quickly review the philosophies of both authorities.

Abraham Maslow is known for his "Hierarchy of Needs" which identifies the five tiers of human needs. These tiers include Physiological, Safety, Belonging, Esteem, and Self-actualization. Simply stated these tiers of basic human needs. Students cannot fully meet the expectations of school if they do not have adequate sleep, clothing, exercise and other physical or bodily needs. As the student moves up the hierarchy, once the essential basic needs are met, he moves into self-actualization and self-esteem. These two tiers consist of confidence, achievement and respect. I believe one will be able to identify Maslow's theory as they read some of the following stories.

Research suggests that once Maslow's tiers are achieved, the teacher and student can then concentrate on Benjamin Bloom's Taxonomy of Educational Objectives. Bloom's Taxonomy organizes the cognitive skills for learning. He labels those skills as knowledge, comprehension, application, analysis, synthesis and evaluation. There are revised publications of Bloom's Taxonomy but essentially these are the cognitive levels I have used in my work with students and teachers. Essentially, students move up Bloom's pyramid by not just learning new material but learning how to analyze the information as well as apply it. I tend to identify that as "owning the learning". They don't just memorize the material but it becomes a part of who they are. Teachers today frequently use Bloom's Taxonomy to develop lesson plans and design assessments.

The phrase *Maslow before Bloom* is popular in education circles. It is typically used to communicate how humans require their basic needs being met before academic learning can be fully embraced. With students now experiencing *school-at-home* during this COVID-19 epidemic, we all may gain some insight from this phrase *Maslow before Bloom. (Mullen, 2020).*

Chapter 1

Introduction

Many of the stories that I will share come from my teaching at the elementary level, some from my administrative experience and some from my work as an educational consultant with an Educational Service Center.

This story has been a long time in the writing. For years I have wanted to share my message about the role of educators as it relates to the lives of students. It truly is about "teaching" and "learning". I struggled with where to begin and what to say as well as to whom I might say it. Furthermore, I didn't know if anyone would even want to hear it. As time has passed and I have continued to work with educators I have become more determined than ever to "tell my story", as the saying goes. I want to tell the story of my passion for the worth of each and every child that enters the classroom doors. I believe that to every child there is a key. And there are as many different keys as there are doors in the schoolhouse. If that key that would open a student's willingness to connect with school is not readily apparent, are we to just walk away? Would we walk away if we couldn't find the right key to our house or our car? NO. We would keep searching and searching and getting help if that's what was required. But we would NEVER walk away. So must we never give up on finding just the right key to any child with whom we have been given the opportunity to know and to teach. We must be prepared to invest the time, effort and money necessary to do whatever it takes to ensure a successful future for all children. Do I believe that those who chose education as a profession believe that EVERY KID COUNTS? Of course, they want to ensure success for every child. However, the concept of "Every Child" is huge and seems unrealistic to many. I also find that complacency, frustration and lack of support overshadow what should be the forefront of the system called "education". As I moved into administration and felt the overwhelming responsibility for a large number of students I came to accept EVERY KID COUNTS as my professional philosophy. It's simply stated but extremely challenging and complex in practice. We must recognize that no child can be forgotten, ignored, or left behind in the formative years. What we, as educators, do or do not do on a daily basis will undeniably impact the future of these young people.

We've all read, seen or heard about the endless number of books written by experts that discuss schools and what would make a difference and contribute to the success of all kids. The research regarding that success is clear but we don't seem to get the job done. I'm not sure why that is. Is it because we don't know what "ensuring success for all kids" looks like, feels like or sounds like? It is usually just those reform trailblazers that are willing to step out and try something new. A lot of "how to" books have been written describing strategies for ensuring success for all students. Those books, written by "experts" try to explain ways to do "what's right for kids". I heard Ray McNulty at a conference once say, "I can give you all the ingredients you need to build a successful school but if you don't have the passion or commitment, it still won't yield the results you're looking for". (Raymond J. McNulty, Past President of the International Center for Leadership in Education)

The inability to put new ideas into practice is called the knowing-doing gap. It is a widely used expression that is not unique to education; it is taught in college courses, a vital part of leadership training, and is a mainstay in the world of business. In the words of Dale Carnegie, 'Knowledge isn't power until it is applied.' In their book, *The Knowing-Doing Gap: How Smart Companies Turn Knowledge Into Action*, authors Jeffrey Pfeffer and Robert Sutton explain that some people are "drowning in a sea of good intentions" because they spend an inordinate amount of time talking about an idea ("word spinning") instead of making any progress. They state that "the gap between knowing and doing is more important than between ignorance and knowing." According to the authors, some people delude themselves into thinking they are making progress simply because they keep talking about the idea. In order to move a plan into the action stage, they caution that a plan may get derailed early on if there are too many details in the beginning. They further endorse the practice of celebrating "moments of excitement" as a plan unfolds. It is likewise important to not spend time focusing on snags that may occur and to focus on what worked instead. (Just Ask Publication, June 2017)

I don't think my story is any different from the books I've read, or at least my beliefs are no different from the beliefs about which I've read. Maybe if I talk about where I've seen those beliefs put into practice and seen how they made a difference for **real kids** and **real teachers** in **real schools** the message will seem more clear and the reality seem more like a possibility. If my book is different in any way, it will be in the sharing of personal stories and personal beliefs about the teaching profession. These stories come from the challenges that I've faced and the outstanding educators whom I've had the pleasure of knowing.

Organizing my ramblings in a way that would make sense to the reader was a bit of a challenge. It took a great deal of soul searching to be able to articulate my passion for children and what I believe about the power of teachers. I chose to examine and organize my beliefs into some sort of logical order and then share my student stories within those areas. The areas that I've chosen to discuss in my book are **real kids, real teachers** and **real schools.** While these areas obviously overlap, I've attempted to address each on its own merits.

As I share stories about real kids I will talk about the unmistakable significance of building a school culture, forming relationships, setting high expectations, making connections and teaching to the students' strengths. It behooves us to help students see that school has something to offer them.

In the section that talks about real teachers you will read stories about teachers that have the passion, dedication and understanding about what it takes to truly make a difference in the lives of students. I shall attempt to convey the importance of collective capacity.

The last section will discuss how schools have established a climate for learning and created a culture in which all stakeholders share a common belief, vision and mission for their school community. It's easy to get bogged down in those clichés around the terms "belief", "vision", "mission". I wish I could remember where I once read a metaphor that might help to put those three words in perspective. Nevertheless, it went something like this:

> A belief might be that there is indeed extraterrestrial life.
> The vision would be the ability to explore space to prove that theory.
> The mission then becomes doing whatever is necessary to build the vessel which could take us there.

Compare that to a school environment:

> If our belief is that every kid counts and that every kid can learn.
> Our vision would be a school that is organized in a manner that ensures every child does indeed learn and is indeed successful in school.
> Our mission becomes doing whatever is necessary to build a system that would ensure that success. Now that is a challenge.

Chapter 1

The Journey Begins

My story as an educator begins when I was just a child who loved to play with dolls and set up schoolrooms. I especially loved my dolls if they had broken limbs or were ragged and old. I think it was because I thought they needed a little special attention. This love for teaching continued into my later years. I would frequently volunteer to teach Sunday School lessons. We had what was referred to as "Little Church" where youth attended while "Big Church" was in session. I would participate during worship by telling bible stories, using props like a flannel board and flannel characters. I would prepare and practice my lesson throughout the week at home in the evenings. As I became a young woman about to graduate high school in the late 1960's I would earn the honor of becoming the first generation in my family to go to college and I had already decided that teaching was my calling. I found it affirming in my later career as a teacher to discover that term "calling" in the book by Elaine K. McEwan, *Ten Traits of Highly Effective Teachers*.

You may wonder whether this first trait of highly effective teachers should include the concept of *calling* or possibly doubt that people actually feel a calling to teach. The term is often used in educational literature, however, and many of the teachers whom I interviewed in preparation for this book used the term to describe their own feelings of passion for the profession. (McEwan, 2002, p. 27)

To continue with my story, my parents were so proud and so determined to help me but did not have the financial resources to do so. I was fortunate to be awarded a scholarship from the local teachers' association that would help support the cost of attending the nearby teachers' college. I worked part-time and applied for federal assistance known as a National Defense Education loan. As I entered the program to become a teacher and learned more about the opportunities for becoming an educator I received yet another calling. This was a calling that led me to children with whom many educators would not care to work. I was raised in a very small community and was not familiar with the concept of Special Education. As I researched this concept and took classes in that department I became convinced that I wanted to work with special needs children. When questioned by friends and family about my decision to take this route, I would share my belief that every child deserves to be educated to the degree to which they are capable of learning. My best friend and roommate for four years said, "But, Charyll, those kids won't be able to go to college or do the things we've had the opportunities to do." I explained that it was my potential and the potential of those around me to pursue higher education but the potential of some young people might be to become self-reliant and work in a sheltered workshop setting and it was important to me to help them reach that potential. In other words, it is important that they feel successful. Thus began my career as a special educator working with mentally handicapped students.

Questions to ponder:
- Why become a teacher?
- Why does knowledge of what needs to be done so frequently fail to result in action or behavior that is consistent with that knowledge? (Pfeffer & Sutton, 2000, pg. 4)

Chapter 3

Real Kids

We understand the reality that every child comes to us as a blank slate upon which we have the opportunity to help etch their future. Well, I guess the slate isn't totally blank because they have had five years of experiences that have contributed to carving out their future previous to entering school, five years of nurturing. The environment from which they come might have been full of printed text, rich vocabulary and a feeling of love and community. However, the environment may have been void of print, may have provided limited vocabulary and perhaps even created a feeling of uncertainty and disorganization. It is not our responsibility to judge that environment but only to recognize the diversity that five-year olds bring to us as they begin their school career.

> Children from families living in poverty or in households in which parent education is low typically enter school with lower levels of foundational skills, such

as those in language, reading, and mathematics. On starting kindergarten, children in the lowest socio-economic group have average cognitive scores that are 60 percent below those of the most affluent group. Explained largely by socioeconomic differences among ethnic groups, average math achievement is 21 percent lower for African American children than for white children and 19 percent lower for Hispanic children than for non-Hispanic white children. Moreover, due to deep-seated equity issues present in communities and schools, such early achievement gaps tend to *increase* rather than diminish over time. (NAEYC, 2009, p.3)

We must respect the wide range of developmental levels, both behavioral and cognitive. (Again recognizing Maslow before Bloom.) We must, as they say, "meet them where they are". Again, we cannot think that a "one size fits all" philosophy will ensure success for every child.

After I graduated from Emporia State Teachers College it would take no time at all to realize that teaching was so very much more than knowing content and how to deliver that content in a format that would meet every child at their individual cognitive level. How did I learn that lesson? The following stories are examples of how I came to understand that working with children was not just possessing a strong pedagogy or command of the science of teaching. It is so very much more than that. It was also about forming relationships, setting high expectations for all students, making connections and teaching to the students' strengths.

One morning early in October of my first teaching assignment in an old two-story building "Gary's" father came to visit with me because he felt I needed to know what had happened to Gary earlier that morning. Now this dad worked nights at a local tire manufacturing plant and he and his co-workers were known to frequent a local bar when they finished their shift at 7:00 in the morning. I detected that had been the case this particular morning but evidently he felt it was still important that he come to school to share some important information with Gary's teacher. His conversation was as follows: "I just need to let you know that when Gary was getting ready for school this morning he caught his private parts in his zipper and I think he may not be in a very good mood today." (Gary had a struggle controlling his behavior when he reached a high level of frustration. I respected his dad for recognizing this character trait of Gary's and knowing that it was important for those working with Gary to know his state of mind when he came to school.) It became abundantly clear to me at that point that I was inexperienced because I was somewhat speechless, not to mention embarrassed. But I also recognized that Gary's dad did not view me as young, inexperienced or embarrassed but as Gary's teacher who would want and need to know this information if she were to have a successful day with his son. The best response I had at that point was, "Thank you for the information and I want to encourage you to come visit with me any time you have information that might help me as I work with your son, Gary."

My next wakeup call came from my paraprofessional who had raised children of her own and had all the "common sense" about children that I was obviously lacking. Again, my youth and inexperience were abundantly clear as I constantly searched for information regarding the use of paraprofessionals. I felt only moderately competent to deal with students, let alone another adult in my classroom. I was the "teacher" but she had experience that enabled her to identify student needs that were not necessarily academic.

This is one case in point. "Miranda" consistently had a case of bad breath. I didn't have a clue that this could be a medical issue. I thought it was hygienic in nature. My paraprofessional, "Susan", suggested that Miranda might have bad tonsils. "Really?" I thought. I had no idea this could be the cause of the chronic bad breath. I ignored this issue until Miranda continued to miss school due to illness and the bad breath only worsened over time. I finally gave in and went out on a limb with the mother and asked if Miranda had ever been diagnosed with bad tonsils. The answer was "No" but she said she would make an appointment for Miranda with her doctor. Again, if approached in a positive and concerned manner, parents will trust and follow suggestions presented by their student's teacher. As it turned out, Miranda's tonsils were badly infected and, in fact, had to be removed. WOW! It was pretty clear that I had much to learn.

These two experiences taught me very quickly that parents send their children to school under the assumption that they will be cared for in all domains of their lives. Most parents trust us as educators to do what we need to do to help their children. And they also assume that we would not "leave any of them behind". No Child Left Behind is an outdated law but still a term I have not forgotten and consistently use in my work with teachers. In my position as an educational consultant, I provided training to numerous educators on a daily basis and one of my standard comments went like this, "If we are going to leave a child behind, whose child will that be? It's not going to be my child or my grandchild. Can it be your child or your grandchild?" We need to re-member that every one of the children with whom we work belongs to someone who expects us not to leave their child behind. In reality that is a daunting task.

I would spend the next twenty-one years teaching in special education and general education classrooms. I began teaching special needs stu-dents just as Public Law 94-142 and Individual Education Plans came into existence. Public Law 94-142 (Education of All Handicapped Children Act) that was passed by Congress in 1975 is now better known as IDEA, Individuals with Disabilities Education Act and comes under Public Law 108-446. It is a federal law that assures free and public education to all children with disabilities. It was around 1970 when teachers first experienced the challenge of writing Individ-ual Education Plans (IEP's) for all children identified as a student with one or more disabilities. The pendulum for delivery of services for these students has swung from totally self-contained classes with a spe-cial educator to self-contained with some inclusion (mainstreaming) in a general education setting to total inclusion in the general educa-tion setting with little or no support from the special educator. The pendulum has continued to swing from one extreme to the opposite over my forty years in the field. Consequently, the concept of Least Restrictive Environment became the new guideline for services deliv-ered to the special education student. "Least restrictive environment" means that a student with an identified disability should have the opportunity to be educated with non-disabled peers, to whatever degree appropriate. They should have access to any program or activity that non-disabled peers would be able to access.

After my first thirteen years or so as a special educator I wanted to experience a general education classroom. During this time, I was attending the university in an effort to obtain my Masters Degree in administration. I was fortunate enough to secure a position in a general education setting in the building to which I was already assigned. I had the opportunity to teach first, second, third and sixth grades. It was interesting to note that students in my sixth-grade classroom, that I had also taught in first grade, truly did not change much. What I found was that the same affective demeanor that first graders demonstrated was also present as they moved into sixth grade. They may get taller and their physical characteristics may mature but the "kid within" doesn't change much. They just are who they are.

> Our personalities stay pretty much the same throughout our lives, from our early childhood years to after we're over the hill, according to a new study. The results show personality traits observed in children as young as first graders are a strong predictor of adult behavior. (Live Science, 2010)

When I moved into an administrative position, I had an At-Risk school, kindergarten through eighth grade. At-Risk might be identified as a community of students from low socio-economic situations or perhaps a higher than normal number of special needs students or students that lived in drug-infested and/or crime-ridden environments. My next assignment would be in an affluent Pre-K through sixth grade building with the district's Early Childhood Program. Many of the stories that follow will refer to those two settings. During that same time period I also raised two daughters who attended public school and throughout this book I will share not only experiences of my students but those of my daughters as well. Through my stories of real kids and real teachers the reader will have the opportunity to begin to recognize how my passions for and beliefs in the role of educators in the lives of children evolved.

How do really masterful teachers work with students in a way that translates into success for those students? I believe it is through forming relationships, setting high expectations, making connections, establishing a nurturing culture and teaching to the students' strengths. Let me begin to share ways that teachers go about doing that work and some stories that will clearly illustrate those essential components of effective teaching.

My awareness of the impact that teachers have on the lives of those students with whom they work grew rapidly as the years rolled by. Year after year I would consciously work to establish strong relationships with my students and their parents. I, like any person standing in classrooms today, have endless stories about the daily opportunities to either make "deposits" or "withdrawals" in the lives of children.

> Covey (1989) uses the notion of an emotional bank account to convey the crucial aspects of relationships. He indicates that in all relationships one makes deposits to and withdrawals from the other individual in that relationship. The following chart is just one example of deposits and withdrawals. (Payne, 2013, p.102-103.)

DEPOSITS	WITHDRAWALS
Seek first to understand	Seeks first to be understood
Keeping promises	Breaking promises
Kindnesses, courtesies	Unkindnesses, discourtesies
Clarifying expectations	Violating expectations
Loyalty to the absent	Disloyalty, duplicity
Apologies	Pride, conceit, arrogance
Open to feedback	Rejecting feedback

Adapted from Stephen Covey, *The Seven Habits of Highly Effective People*

Let's examine this concept for a minute. I cannot say that I was always on the left side of this chart but I want to share some experiences that might further demonstrate what happens to students that are consistently having deposits or withdrawals made on their self esteem and self image.

My husband and I were out at a party one night and this very handsome and polite young man comes up and inquires about who I might be. He asked if I was Mrs. Boggs. Now, at my age, I have learned that this question indicates that this is indeed a former student or parent. I didn't immediately recognize this young man. When he told me his name, I remembered an ornery little guy who had established quite a reputation for himself. In fact, most teachers did not care to have "J.P." in their classes. Our conversation follows.

"You were always my favorite teacher," J.P. commented.

I said, "Sure, J.P., I'm your favorite teacher because I happen to be the one in front of you at this particular moment."

He replied, quite seriously, "You know why you were my favorite teacher? It's because you always told me that I was OK and that when

I grew up I was going to be successful and have a great life. You said I was a good kid and would do great things one day. And you were right, I am doing just fine in my life. I just need to thank you for that."

He went on to share what he was doing as an adult. I was speechless at that moment so I just replied, "Thank you J.P. and you know I guess I was right because you are a fine young man. You need to know that I'm very proud of you."

Now, I don't recall making that "deposit" into J.P.'s young life, but I do remember his situation and I do remember the many withdrawals that were made from his emotional bank account on a daily basis. I remember the many teachers that "wrote J.P. off" before he ever got to their classroom. We've all seen those kinds of stereotyping situations where a child is judged by his skin, clothes, parents or past deeds. While I didn't recall having said those exact words, I do know that I tried to recognize each and every student for who they were and what they had to offer. I tried to connect with them on an authentic level. Not some fake connection because kids will see right through such a façade.

Another very sad example involves one of my daughters. My younger daughter's experiences with the "system" were, without a doubt, genuine examples of what might happen to students who have few deposits and innumerable withdrawals made to their student-school emotional bank account. Her story is not unlike the story of many, many children in our classrooms today. She was what I consider a victim of trying to make her fit the mold of the system instead of the system considering her needs and utilizing her strengths to help her reach her potential. During her time in the system the practice for struggling students was to group them for the purpose of "helping" all of those struggling students at the same time. Another word for this practice was "tracking". I worked diligently as a mother and teacher to help her find success in the "one size fits all" mold. And while we studied for hours on end, did homework together, communicated with the school regularly and graduated from high school by acquiring all of the required credit hours, she was not able to reach her potential through the system as it existed in the late 1980's. Let me tell you the story of my daughter and her experiences as a student. Now that I am older, wiser and have had time to reflect I am able to articulate her school career in the following story.

Even in first grade it was obvious that Dana was developmentally less mature than her peers and regularly experienced negative consequences for not finishing her reading assignments as quickly as the other students. That consequence frequently was to sit alone in the classroom during recess as a punishment for not having completed her assigned work in the allotted time and receive negative marks on her report card. She frequently questioned why her teacher didn't like her. Why would a five-year-old have the impression that her teacher, this person who is so important in her life, would not like her? Why did this teacher feel it necessary to "make withdrawals" from Dana's emotional bank account? Now I have to say that I don't want to believe there is a teacher alive who deliberately or consciously makes "withdrawals from a student's emotional bank account". I would rather believe it was lack of training or experience or understanding that resulted in those "withdrawals". It was not until she entered second grade that a very conscientious and attentive teacher met with Dana's father and me to discuss her concerns about Dana's maturity and ability to meet success in the system as it was designed. This quality teacher did what she could to support Dana and provided opportunities for her to learn and grow academically. But this teacher was an exception to most of those Dana would encounter throughout her school career. Because she got off to such a rough start during those beginning years when students are learning to read and forming a positive relationship with school, she never seemed to totally recover. Her self-esteem was damaged and her love for learning just never happened.

I have come to understand and believe that it is those early years in public education that mold a child's future in this process we call education. I found my first and second graders to be like little sponges who soaked up all the new learnings put before them. They had no history of failure and didn't see themselves as failures. If they can experience success in those early formative years, they will be "hooked" into the learning process and even if it takes a little longer for some to master a concept, they will believe they can learn and achieve. On who or what does that depend? We all know… it is the classroom teacher who establishes a learning environment that differentiates instruction and is dedicated to ensuring success for each and every student.

Dana's feeling of low self-worth was only perpetuated by an experience that she had with a Drill Team sponsor at the high school. We tried to get her involved in some group that would recognize her strengths and ultimately boost her self-esteem. She was able to be involved with such a group, sponsored by the school and sought after by many. She was a talented and beautiful young lady and easily made this team her freshman year. Her sister, her closest friend at the time, had been on the team for a year and mentored her sister as they both tried out for the upcoming year. Both girls were successful in their tryouts and went on to perform together for that year. When her older sister graduated and left for college, Dana felt lost and alone. Both girls had been involved in the same performance group, Dana saw her sister and her sister's friends as role models. She began to lose interest in the group and started skipping meetings. This caused her to lose points and consequently be banned from performing with the group. I understood the process and did not question the consequence. However, Dana's father and I requested a meeting with the sponsor and principal. Our conversation went as follows. My question to the sponsor was "Do you see yourself as a disciplinarian or mentor to the young people with whom you work?" Her answer was fairly immediate and held an air of little genuine concern for students and their self esteem, "I see my role as a disciplinarian." My reply was "That's sad. You, as an adult in the school, have the opportunity to mentor young adults as they go through difficult transitions and look toward the future as an adult citizen. But you seem to believe they are on their own and poor decisions mean they are out of the group and not worthy of your time or worthy of being a member of the group any longer. I feel badly that you have chosen to have that type of relationship with your students." The meeting was over as she made her final comment, "Well, that's how I see my role." Again, there were withdrawals being made to Dana's emotional bank account. As a side note, it was interesting that the principal had no comment. It became perfectly clear that he also did not view the role of high school teachers or sponsors as mentors for the adolescents with whom they worked. Again, I can't believe that these withdrawals are made with malice. It just seems to be the way our educational institutions have developed over the years. We seem to have forgotten the need that all, including our youth, have for acceptance and positive relationships. Students are not always viewed as humans with genuine feelings that they often cannot recognize or explain and I see adults as the folks who can mentor and listen to those young people when they feel safe enough to talk about their feelings, fears, and concerns.

While my daughter was unfortunate to have so many withdrawals made to her emotional bank account, I must also share our experience with a person who, on the contrary, always demonstrated a caring demeanor toward Dana. This special person was a counselor, not her "assigned" counselor but someone with whom she had made a connection. She would say, "Mom, if I leave a note for "Mrs. Caresalot" she may not get back to me on the same day but she ALWAYS gets back to me." I called Mrs. Caresalot the next day and said, "You don't need to tell me what you and Dana talk about, I just wanted to thank you for being there for her. It gives me peace of mind to know that she has someone she can go to in a place where she has little opportunity to feel worthy. It means so much to me and I know it means the world to her. I just wanted to say Thank You." I am sure this woman is a major reason why Dana was able to complete her high school education.

Much has been researched, documented and written regarding setting expectations for students. Students will always rise to the expectations put upon them. If the expectation is for poor behavior and low achievement, they will indeed not disappoint us. Most of us might remember the TESA Program, Teacher Expectation Student Achievement.

TESA, or Teacher Expectations and Student Achievement, was developed in the 1970s. It has been tried and true and has been recognized as one of the finest training programs available to all teachers and administrators. TESA training focuses on changing teacher behavior, not student behavior, because much of the expected success of students is a direct result of how teachers respond to specific students in the classroom. If a teacher believes a student is a high achiever, he/she may direct higher-thinking-level questions to that child. On the contrary, if a teacher believes a student is more of a low achiever, he/she may subconsciously direct easier questions to that student. Consequently that student may be successful but at a lower cognitive level.

> The basis for the original development of TESA was the empirical question: *If teachers practiced specific motivating and supportive interactions more frequently with low achievers, would statistically significant academic growth result?* A three-year external validation study was conducted, and findings determined that approximately 2,000 low-achieving students in experimental classes showed statistically significant academic gains over their counterparts in control classes. In addition, significant reductions in absenteeism and discipline referrals were found. Results of this research led to the formation of the TESA model. (bpslearningsessions, 2004, p. 3.)

> The link between success in a given endeavor and our belief in our ability to succeed is well established. In education, a growing body of research indicates that the belief system of teachers heavily influences their students' possibilities of success. In short, "Positive expectations yield positive results". (Failure is Not an Option, Blankstein, 2004, pg. 17-18)

How do we ensure successful learning for all students? Most educators are trying very hard and come to their work with a genuine desire to succeed with each of their students. However, there are undeniably numerous significant obstacles to learning. These include, but are not limited to, differing learning styles, need for additional time and repetition, low socioeconomic status, a language other than English spoken in the home, parent/family situations that interfere with the learning process. In high-performing schools, these variables are addressed in a proactive manner so they do not become barriers to the successful achievement of all students. Teachers are engaged in continuous study of educational research to learn how to prevent failure and how to provide effective interventions for each student in need. They actively seek alternatives to failure, and the concept of 'throw-away' students is itself discarded. (Blankstein, 2004, p. 98).

Throughout my career I have seen many professionals who expect students to come to school ready to follow the rules and regulations and meet the expectations put upon them by the institution. Why would we think that? Why do we think that student compliance automatically happens? How many of us, as adults, do something without reason or motivation? Very few, I suspect. Why would we expect anything different from children? If children don't see that school has anything to offer them why would we expect them to comply with the expectations of the system? As the educators, we need to set expectations while helping students to recognize the result of meeting those expectations. In other words, helping students to answer the question, "What's in it for me?" "T.J" is a prime example of needing to know what school had to offer him. T.J. came to me as a middle school student. He had already taken a home-made bomb to his previous school and it didn't take long for me to figure out that he was a very bright child. But he was having trouble finding success in school. He was the type of kid that if there weren't something in it for him he wasn't interested or engaged. I had tried several different strategies with T.J. when he would become stubborn and uncooperative with his teachers. I tried the old "You know, T.J., if you don't take care of your school responsibilities as a middle school student, you won't be able to go to the high school." His all too familiar response would be, "Oh, well." And he meant it! I knew from the start that the threat of promotion or lack there of was not going to be an effective strategy when working with T.J. Going to the high school or not going to the high school was of no real consequence in his book. I was fortunate enough to have assembled a terrific middle school team. They were truly dedicated to the students and to the future of those students. T.J.'s teachers and I started working diligently to establish a relationship with him, finding out what was important to him, finding out where his strengths did indeed lie. To exemplify the notion that some students really need to feel that school has something to offer them before they can become engaged in the process let me share the story about finding the hook that would engage T.J.

My middle school students participated in our league Quiz Bowl competitions on Fridays for about nine weeks. We had figured out that T.J. had a great deal of general knowledge, knowledge that many of his peers did not appear to possess. We investigated the possibility of putting T.J. on the school Quiz Bowl team. He was hesitant (lacked confidence) but was willing to give it a try. His peers readily recognized him as a huge asset to the team and T.J. was proud to have found an area in which he could excel. During the weeks when T.J. was not getting his work handed in his teachers would give him reminders like, "Gosh, T.J., if you're behind on Friday, you aren't going to be able to go to the Quiz Bowl". Or comments like, "Your team really needs you; they really need you on the team. So, what can I do to help you out here?" The teachers were great with him. They would stay after school, give up their plan times, do whatever it took to keep T.J. engaged in the learning process. While he had the ability to keep up with his studies, he wasn't accustomed to doing school work. This hook, the Quiz Bowl, engaged T.J. in the learning process. And it provided opportunities for T.J. to experience success and to develop a sense of belonging. We all know that success breeds success. During our time with T.J., we were always challenged to understand where he was coming from and what was and was not priority with him. We worked tirelessly to provide a school setting that was appropriate yet meaningful in T.J.'s world. This setting needed to address student engagement that would lead to academic success. Once teachers could identify T.J.'s strengths and T.J. could experience success in school the teaching and learning process only continued to improve.

That reminds me of the story of another young man I met during my administrative tenure in the middle school. This was a young man with an extraordinarily large amount of anger and frustration with the world in general. His attitude sounded something like this, "I dare you to engage me in this process called school and learning". He and I had to work through several months of long talks, negotiating appropriate behaviors and resulting consequences before we were able to establish a working relationship that resulted in his compliance with the parameters of our school setting and my understanding of his needs while respecting his personal struggles. It became a give and take relationship of mutual respect and understanding. I want to relate one of my "Raylyn" stories as an example of the power that comes when time is taken and energy is expended to form genuine relationships with students.

It was one of those phases when Raylyn was going through a particularly difficult time. This meant that work was not getting completed and classroom behavior was not meeting the expectations of his classroom teachers. When Raylyn would get into one of his downhill slides, it took an inordinate amount of energy and time to get him back on track. This particular time I suggested to one of his teachers, one who had a well-established relationship with Raylyn, that she have a little chat with him. As they were talking about one thing and another he just all of a sudden blurted out, "I can't even take a shower before I come to school because we don't have any water. I know that I stink." Aha! He wasn't saying this in response to any particular question. It was a clue to us about where Raylyn was in his personal life at that particular time. Raylyn was an intelligent and perceptive teenager and of course conscious of the fact that body odor is huge for teenagers. I suggested the teacher let Raylyn know that he could come to school early and use the shower in the locker room. No one else would need to know. Knowledge of his living conditions was important in my relationship with Raylyn and this is why.

One of Raylyn's teachers came to me one day and said, "Raylyn is in the gym shooting baskets and won't return to class". (After lunch the middle school students could have choice time in the gymnasium.) And please note that Raylyn was bigger and stronger than I so physical contact was never an option. I go to the gym and motion to him to come to me.

He gestures back, "Who me?" And I gesture back in an affirmative manner.

He comes over to me and I say, "Hey, buddy, what are you doing?"

"Shooting baskets."

"What are you supposed to be doing?"

"Supposed to be in class."

"So why aren't you in class?"

"Cause I want to shoot baskets."

"Well, you know bud, we've talked about this before, we only have two jobs here at school – our jobs are teaching and learning. We don't flip hamburgers; we don't sell cars. We have teaching and learning, that's what we do here. If you're not going to do your job – and you know your job, your job is the learning part then you might as well not be here. So, if you're not going to do your job I guess I'll just send you on home." (It is important to note here that as an administrator I did not suspend kids from school because suspending them from school was the same as putting them on the streets. They don't belong on the streets, they belong in school, doing their job.)

He looked at me and he said, "Send me home? You mean right now?"

"Yeah, if you're not going to do your job then you just don't need to be here."

Silent tears started to roll down the cheek of this tall, strong, young man. And he said, "But I don't want to go home".

Now, I know this. I know Raylyn doesn't want to go home and I know that school is a safe place for him. It's a happy place for him and he doesn't want to leave. I also knew that threatening him with bad grades or lack of promotion was not going to be a good strategy.

"Well, your other choice would be to go back to class."

"OK, can I go get my shirt?"

"Sure, that would be a good choice."

He gets his shirt and heads off to class. If I had not had a relationship with Raylyn and he had not had a connection to school, if we'd not had an understanding, if he had not trusted me that encounter would not have had a successful resolution. But letting Raylyn know that we had expectations and if he wasn't willing or able to meet those expectations, then school was not the place for him at this time. It made all the difference in the world because he knew I was not threatening, I was not being "mean". It was just a matter of knowing that he had a job to do and if he was not prepared to do that job, there was no need for him to be at school.

Did it take time to build that relationship with Raylyn? Without a doubt, building relationships requires a huge time investment but in the long run everybody's school life is enriched. I always hear that excuse when I am working with teachers, "It takes too much time." However if the time is not invested then the outcome will be a struggle for both the teacher and students for the next nine months. Ultimately the student will not experience the success that is desired for all students and the teacher will not experience a pleasant year of teaching. I also remind them that not all students need that time investment. If there is an extraordinarily large number of students who appear to need that time then perhaps the culture of the classroom needs to be examined.

During my younger daughter, Dana's, high school career, she had few positive experiences. Again, she was in a tracking situation and not offered opportunities to participate in higher level classes or electives in her areas of interest. She never failed a class because together we were able to complete all basic requirements. But it was unbelievably difficult and did little for her self esteem. Consequently, she developed a highly negative attitude toward learning. But let me tell a story about my epiphany about children and recognizing and utilizing their individual strengths. My daughter did some volunteer work one summer at a camp for handicapped students. Many of the students used sign language to communicate and my daughter quickly picked up the skill of signing. That fall she took a class at the local university to learn signing. She only attended class a half a dozen times because her limited time would not allow any time for night classes. It was then that I recognized that all students have strengths and interests but those seem to have no place in the curriculum of typical high schools. This is a girl who had always experienced success when a learning experience was hands on or of interest to her. It was an academic death sentence for her when she was given a paper and pencil task that contained an innumerable amount of words. Reading tasks such as these required matching vocabulary to definitions which had a huge implication about understanding content vocabulary. She rarely was given an opportunity to talk about what she knew or to demonstrate her level of understanding or comprehension in a way other than with a paper/pencil task. I do see high schools from time to time that appear sensitive to such students. They grasp the idea that students don't have to be able to conquer a paper-pencil test to demonstrate their learning.

Another example of the expectations in the world of work as opposed to a typical school setting can also be seen in Dana's first post graduate employment setting.

Her first job after high was computer based and she was trained hands on. She was doing well until time for the first paper-pencil exam She shared her anxiety with her supervisor. Her supervisor assured her that she would be able to pass the exam. Following the exam her supervisor called her in for a conference and asked some questions that were on the exam and she was able to answer those questions. The supervisor shared that, while she had missed some questions on the exam, he was fairly confident from his observations that she was well trained and perfectly capable of doing the job.

The result of my daughter's K-12 experience continues to impact her today in her adult life. The circumstances of my daughter's experience in school only accelerated my passion to do what I could to spread my message about the imperative need to look at students as individuals and find ways to work with them that would lead to a high level of learning. I recognize this is a challenging undertaking. But, again, if we choose to TEACH that means teach each child in the most effective manner available to us and with a passion and determination that won't accept failure of any child to reach their own potential. If we don't have the tools to do that, then we must, as professionals, go in search of those tools through professional development and collaboration with colleagues. We must search relentlessly for the "right key" to each and every child with whom we have been given the opportunity and challenge to teach.

When I arrived at my first administrative assignment I found this very small, very old, almost 100-year-old two story building, I was so excited; I thought it was a dream come true. It took no time at all to recognize this school was located in an extremely At-Risk community. By "at-risk" I mean that the community had data that showed a history of low family income and a high rate of crime. The population was kindergarten through eighth grade. It was during the implementation of the new state-mandated Quality Performance Accreditation system in our state and schools were required to examine all data regarding the school community. We found there were numerous indicators that allowed us to diagnose some of the causes for the low achievement patterns within our school population. Trend data exposed an extremely high retention rate in kindergarten and first grade. Yet the students being retained were not necessarily developmentally delayed or unable to learn, we just found that they were not coming to school "ready to learn". Their early childhood experiences were limited as far as their understanding of literacy, routines, and social interactions. We dedicated our efforts to providing additional time and opportunities for our young students to mature and develop their cognitive abilities. Within the first three years at this school I was fortunate enough to hire some outstanding, highly quality educators who cared as deeply about the success of every child as I did. As educators we had much to learn about possible practices, structures and strategies that would support these at-risk students. After a due amount of study and research we chose to implement a multi-age structure and use developmentally appropriate practice to design the instruction. Together we were able to write a couple of substantially large state grants to implement all day kindergarten and a multi-age structure, kindergarten through eighth grade. We were able to study the concept of developmentally appropriate practices and even travel to Maine to visit a school that had been implementing multi-age classrooms for several years. I want to discuss for just a bit what we learned about developmentally appropriate practices and multi-age grouping of students.

Developmentally Appropriate Practice (also known as DAP) is a teaching perspective in early childhood education where a teacher nurtures a child's development (social, emotional, physical, and cognitive). Following are the three areas of knowledge which must be considered by teachers implementing Developmentally Appropriate Practices.

1. <u>What is known about child development and learning</u>
   – referring to knowledge of age-related characteristics
   that permits general predictions about what experiences
   are likely to best promote children's learning and development. Teachers who are knowledgeable about
   child development and learning are able to make broad
   predictions about what children of a particular age
   group typically will be like, what they typically will and
   will not be capable of and what strategies and approaches will most likely promote their optimal learning and development.

2. <u>What is known about each child as an individual</u> – referring to what practitioners learn about each child that
   has implications for how best to adapt and be respon-
   sive to that individual variation. To be effective,
   teachers must get to know each child in the group well.
   They do this using a variety of methods – such as observation, clinical interview (an extended dialogue in
   which the adult seeks to discern the child's concepts or
   strategies), examination of children's work, individual
   child assessments and talking with families.

3. <u>What is known about the social and cultural context in
   which children live</u> – referring to the values, expectations, and behavioral and linguistic conventions that
   shape children's lives at home and in their communities
   that practitioners must strive to understand in order to
   ensure that learning experiences in the program or
   school are meaningful, relevant, and respectful for each
   child and family. When children are in a group setting

outside the home, what makes sense to them, how they use language to interact, and how they experience this new world depend on the social and cultural contexts to which they are accustomed. A skilled teacher takes such contextual factors into account, along with children's ages and their individual differences, in shaping all aspects of the learning environment. (NAEYC, 2009, p. 9-10)

Below are eleven statements that serve a primary definition of the multi-age, continuous-progress approach to school as defined by Anderson and Pavan:

1. Individual differences in the pupil population are accepted and respected, and there is ample variability in instructional approaches to respond to varying needs.
2. Learning, which is the "work" of the child is intended to be not only challenging but also pleasurable and rewarding.
3. Students are viewed as a whole; development in cognitive, physical, aesthetic, social, and emotional spheres is nurtured.
4. The administrative and organizational framework, for example with respect to pupil grouping practices, is flexible and provides opportunities for each child to interact with children, and adults, of varying personalities, backgrounds, abilities, interests, and ages.
5. Students are enabled through flexible arrangements to progress at their own best pace and appropriately varied ways. Instruction, learning opportunities, and movement within the curriculum are individualized to correspond with individual needs,

interests, and abilities.

6. Curricular areas are both integrated and separate. Instructional, programmatic, and organizational patterns are flexible, with outcomes rather than mere coverage of content as the primary focus.

7. The expected standard of performance (in terms of outcomes) in the core areas of the curriculum are clearly defined, so that the points to be reached by the end of a designated period are well known. However, the time taken to reach that end, and the path followed to that end, is allowed to vary for students with different histories and potentialities.

8. Within the curriculum and related assessment practices, specific content learning is generally subordinate to the understanding of major concepts and methods of inquiry, and the development of the skills of learning: inquiry, evaluation, interpretation, and application.

9. Student assessment is holistic, to correspond with the holistic view of learning.

10. Evaluation of the learner is continuous, comprehensive, and diagnostic. Except for reference purposes as necessary to parental and staff understanding, chronological age and grade norms play a much smaller role in evaluation and reporting activities than does the child's own growth history and potential.

11. While there are some core components of the curriculum that are especially valued (as reflected in performance standards in the major content areas), the system is largely teacher-managed and controlled. Thus, it empowers teachers to create learning opportunities and to use instructional strategies at their own discretion, based on the perceived needs of the students they

are serving. Assessment procedures are similarly flexible, individualized, and teacher-managed. (Anderson, Pavan, 1993, p. 62-63)

In David Pratt's opinion, Canadian educator, "multi-age grouping is associated with better self-concept and attitude toward school." In his writings he also discusses children's friendships, levels of competition and aggression, and levels of harmony and nurturance in the two contrasting arrangements. In his view, multi-age situations produce better results in these areas, and also in language development, cognitive growth, social and emotional development, and altruism. (Anderson, Pavan, 1993, p. 98)

"Timmy" is a fine example of what can happen if those who work with children understand and respect Developmentally Appropriate Practice (DAP) and the multi-age structure. Timmy was a small statured little guy who came to us from a family not unlike many who lived in this community. He was familiar with the notion that he would need to take care of himself and hopefully be a survivor in this life. In the coming years there would be home visits made by Social Services and behavioral issues at school. But it didn't take long for those of us who worked with Timmy at school to recognize that "traditional" consequences for inappropriate behaviors were of little consequence to Timmy. He was pretty independent and certainly determined to operate on his own agenda. And his own agenda did not include learning on a predetermined schedule. Timmy had little exposure to print, reading or writing. Nor had he had any other opportunities which could be classified as pre-K skills. Fortunately for Timmy, our staff had been studying DAP and had initiated the multi-age structure for kindergarten-first grade classes.

While Timmy was consistently reluctant to meet the typical expectations to learn about letters, sounds, numbers or handwriting, he did enjoy "writing" in his journal. Early in the year I visited Timmy's classroom during a journaling time and I went over to Timmy and asked him to tell me what he was putting in his journal. He said, "It's a car." Now, it is noteworthy to say that his dad spent a great deal of time working on car engines and Timmy had extensive knowledge of the workings of car engines. This "car" in his journal was basically scribbles. I complimented him on his drawing and went on my way. About three months later I again visited during journal time and again checked with Timmy to see what he was putting in his journal. Not surprisingly, he said, "I'm making a car." Then he looked at me and asked, "What else does a car have?" I suggested that he might want to consider a windshield or hood or maybe a trunk. He got pretty excited and said, "Oh, yeah!" and quickly added these features to his drawing. Now his drawings began to take a familiar form as the months passed. Until one day he came to my office to show me what he had put in his journal. He had drawn a very sophisticated picture of a car and had written at the top of the page "1998 Red Cutlass". Oh, my gosh! His teacher said that he had asked what kind of car she had and had also asked how to spell Cutlass. But he had independently written 1998 and red. He could write those because he had heard and seen those numbers and words for months but never had reason to use them until he wanted to say something about his picture.

Now there were several things at work here that need to be pointed out. First of all, Timmy was not "ready" to learn when he came to school. Timmy would not be ready to write words and numbers until he had time to work through the scribbling and drawing stages of development. That is like understanding that babies go through the developmental stages of crawling, standing, walking and then running. Secondly, Timmy had absolutely no vested interest in meeting the expectations of learning. His personality was extremely resistant and as I said earlier, traditional consequences had no impact on his behaviors. He had a great personality and was so easy to like. He was friendly and had a great sense of humor. But it was important for him to use what he knew, in this instance it was cars, to connect with what school had to offer him. And we needed to also use what he knew as well as understand from where he was coming if we were going to move this very bright child further in his education so that he might become a successful and productive citizen.

An interesting addition to Timmy's story is his experience in fourth grade. His teacher was a veteran of teaching and a veteran of what might be considered "old school" where the teacher drives the instruction, not the needs or developmental levels of students. I could foresee a train wreck on the horizon. Just as a little additional background, the fourth and fifth grade teachers were the last to join the multi-age concept in our building. The primary folks were well supported and were prepared to implement the multi-age format. Even the 6th-8th grade teachers were anxious to try some multi-age groupings within their content areas.

We talked to the fourth-grade teacher, "Mrs. Myway", and tried to head off the train wreck. Well, surprisingly, I had underestimated Mrs. Myway. She taught Timmy to read using her husband's old editions of *Popular Mechanics*. Now, Mrs. Myway had been through our study of developmentally appropriate practices and multi-age structures and had four years to prepare for students just like Timmy. She was one who first had to see proof of its effectiveness before believing it would work. Some folks operate under the premise that first I believe and then I experience success and some have to experience the success before they can believe. Mrs. Myway saw how the work of those before her produced success and then believed she could also experience that success and sure enough she did.

As we moved ahead with the innovations of multi-age and all-day kindergarten, we encountered many, many struggles, not the least of which was the challenge of change within the community. This change to a multi-age format meant putting younger students with older students and helping folks to understand that this was a research-based and fundamentally sound practice. It was my responsibility to help parents understand that it would benefit the older students as well as the younger ones. The older students are positive role models for the younger students. Older students begin to "own" their learning through teaching others. That teaching might be either academic or behavior focused. The younger students learn procedures, routines and academic skills more rapidly when they can experience them on a daily basis.

Fortunately, our staff had the support of one another, the school board, the state, and many influential patrons. Transitioning to a new way of doing business was a major challenge. While the plans were designed on research-based best practices, many parents were skeptical of the change.

What is so frequently lacking in letters or newsletters sent from the principal's office is an explanation as to why this particular decision has been made by the principal and staff. Parents are much more likely to accept a decision they do not favor if an attempt has been made to give a background of the issue and the reasoning that influenced the recommendation. (Anderson, Pavan, 1993, p. 169)

Questions to ponder:
- Why is Timmy a prime example of the need to recognize the concept of DAP?
- How did the multi-age format work in Timmy's case?
- Why not utilize how students learn and design projects so that the students are able to demonstrate their learning in a manner meaningful to them?
- Why does the world of work recognize the benefit of hands-on learning and the value of modifying expectations to meet the learning styles of individuals better than the school environment?
- What gets in the way of recognizing, respecting and responding to the strengths, interests and needs of our students?

Chapter 4

Real Teachers

It was during that era of change in this small school that I saw teachers working long hard hours to meet the needs of students that came from very dysfunctional environments. Many of the families had issues regarding their relationship with school and struggled to recognize any value in such a system. But the staff built in celebrations, rewards and incentives for students and their accomplishments: academically, socially and behaviorally to the level that my belief in the potential of educators to help each and every child reach their individual potential was renewed. My time as principal of this small K-8 building was several years of learning, growing and becoming more passionately dedicated to the success of each and every child. The greatest evidence of that growth lies in the stories of these teachers.

I had always thought I wouldn't mind teaching high school or elementary school but never had a great desire to teach middle school, yet here I was, administrator of an elementary through middle school population. As the first year rolled along, I had many learning opportunities as I became familiar with the community, the families and the children and truly saw that the children were "at risk". They were at risk of failing in school, at risk for alcohol and drug abuse, at risk for physical and psychological abuse in the home. I began to wonder what I had gotten myself into. Some of the experiences included students smoking on the fire escape or getting angry and kicking pencil sharpeners off the wall or cursing at the teachers and telling them just where they could go with their rules and expectations. It didn't take long for me to recognize that drastic changes were in order. As I moved from my first year into my second, I was fortunate to have the opportunity to make some significant changes in the teaching staff. I was able to hire some quality teachers who had the passion for teaching middle level students and certainly had the skills to teach the required content. As we worked together to design the upcoming year, we were able to put some expectations in place that would be new to our students but would begin to establish a climate for learning, as well as a culture of respect for one another, as well as for those in authority.

Our middle school was sixth grade through the eighth grade. We, as a staff, wrote a handbook for middle school students. While we were a kindergarten through eighth grade facility, we functioned more like an elementary and middle school. School expectations were consistent but there were some issues specific to older students due to the nature of middle school age students. We had issues around athletics, Quiz Bowl events, and other extra-curricular activities as well as consideration for the complicated developmental issues faced by these pre-teen students. One of the very specific expectations established was a zero tolerance policy for profanity and fighting. Those were really the only two infractions that would cause a student to have to serve an in-school suspension.

It was our policy to not use out of school suspensions because we strongly believed that students belonged in school doing their job. To suspend them from school only caused them to be out of school and on the streets and we wanted students to be in school. It didn't take long for us to discover that being eligible or ineligible to play sports was not a significant motivator for our students. We knew that there had to be a different consequence for students not meeting the established expectations. We initiated "end-of-the-nine-weeks celebrations". These celebrations had to be events that were extremely meaningful to the students. The celebrations were such events as a trip to the Renaissance Festival, about a hundred miles from their town, or snow skiing at a resort about a hundred and twenty miles away or we would go to the capitol city, about thirty miles away and go to the mall and to a movie. They earned the money to pay for the celebrations by selling cookie dough throughout the community. And the parents that worked outside the community sold it to co-workers. All of the planned events were unfamiliar to these students and they worked diligently to earn their celebrations. What did "earn their celebration" mean? It meant that a student had to pass ALL classes and have no in-school suspensions. Those two expectations covered both the academic and behavioral domains that we felt were of highest priority. While we clearly recognized that inappropriate behaviors may have continued outside the school environment, students had to meet high academic and behavior expectations while at school. Our success rate was about 95% each nine weeks after this new policy was implemented.

I mentioned at the beginning of this book that I had two daughters. My two girls were extraordinarily close but exact opposites when it came to their relationship with the educational process. My elder daughter, Angela, learned quickly how to play the "game of school". And make no doubt, there is a "game" that children must learn if they are to be successful in the system that we have established and so generously call public education for all. Following is Angela's story of school.

While many of Angela's assigned tasks in school meant little to her in her day-to-day life, she knew that she must memorize dates, places and people in order to obtain an acceptable letter grade. As she reached her senior year in high school, she had the opportunity to take some college prep classes that peaked her interest in learning, specifically in the area of composition. Once her interest was peaked, she experienced a high level of success. She began to enjoy writing and began to produce quality work in this area. Angela also had the good fortune to meet instructors at the college level that recognized the various strengths of students and provided opportunities for their students to grow and learn as young adults.

Angela went on to become a teacher, instructional coach and currently is a building administrator. But my daughter is not what I would call a "typical" teacher. She has the strength and confidence to do what needs to be done for each child and puts the grade level standards second. She has come to recognize that if a teacher does not first recognize the needs of each child but simply presents content material in a "one size fits all" format, many students will indeed be left behind. She has figured out it is a great deal of work followed by a greater amount of reward to do what needs to be done to meet the needs of all of those students year after year. Following is Angela's story of "Isaiah". Hopefully it illustrates her exceptionality in working with students. This is the story of Isaiah.

Angela shared with me that when Isaiah's mom brought him to her fourth-grade classroom for the first time he started jumping around the classroom and getting into everything. These were behaviors of perhaps a two-year old as opposed to a fourth-grade student. His mom shared that she didn't believe his needs were being met at his previous school and she demonstrated a hostile and frustrated attitude. His mom had decided after his last IEP meeting (Special Education's Individual Education Plan) that he needed to have a fresh start in a fourth-grade classroom, not a self-contained special education classroom, which was where he had previously been placed.

Angela very quickly observed that Isaiah could not do fourth grade reading or math. His misbehavior was his way of saying he was frustrated and he was compensating by acting out. He refused to line up with the class to go anywhere. It didn't matter whether it was for P.E., music, recess or any activity outside of the classroom.

Angela's next step was to call his previous school to inquire about their strategy for working with Isaiah. Before I share what appeared to be happening in Isaiah's previous school, I want to again say that I don't believe teachers want students to fail or be unsuccessful, I just believe they are doing what they know or have been instructed to do. Maya Angelou is noted for many wise sayings. One of those is "Do the best you can until you know better and when you know better then do better". The previous school shared that they tried to mainstream him (include him in a general education classroom) and he hadn't transitioned well at all. He would have a "meltdown" and the teacher would send him out of the room. He wasn't being held accountable for doing anything. He spent the majority of his days being angry and then going through a cooling off phase, never doing anything that resembled academics. All of the attention and time was spent dealing with behavior.

Angela recognized her first order of business would be to get the behavior and compliance issues under control, as well as creating an environment where Isaiah would feel safe. (Maslow before Bloom) She began by making it clear that she expected him to sit, just sit quietly and listen. She would put him on the computer with headphones doing something that he could do, like first grade math or reading game so that he would not be disruptive. She knew that there were no viable alternatives outside her classroom that would be appropriate options for Isaiah. From what she learned from the previous school and what he had demonstrated when she attempted to send him with his special education provider, she knew her classroom was going to be the best option for Isaiah.

Angela had to meet Isaiah where he was developmentally and academically. She had to find out what he could do independently and feel successful. She had access to a paraprofessional for about three hours during different times throughout the day. Isaiah would respond to the paraprofessional fairly well if she were in the classroom along side of Angela. Angela had to work with the paraprofessional to make sure she didn't push too hard with him. While she wanted him to behave she didn't want him pushed to the point of frustration. After the behavior was under control, they could work on academics. Eventually he showed that he didn't want to be different, he didn't want to be pulled from the classroom. I asked how he demonstrated to her that he didn't want to be different. She told me that he didn't want to go with the paraprofessional or the special education teacher. He literally wouldn't get out of his chair when they came to work with him. He would stare Angela down like he was ticked at her for even considering the idea of sending him out of her room. Isaiah didn't want to be pulled away from his peers, he didn't want everybody looking at him. He didn't want to be doing something different even though his peers already knew that he was not working on material at the same level.

But again, he couldn't do what the rest of the class was doing. Isaiah would try but couldn't and then he would get frustrated and give up and do nothing. It was a vicious cycle all the time. For quite a long time she had to let him do what he wanted as long as it wasn't interfering with the instruction she was presenting to the rest of the students in the classroom. If she were giving instruction and he would randomly get up and go log-on to the computer, she would let him do that. If she were giving whole group instruction and he would go back to the carpet to look at a book, she would let him do that. As long as he wasn't interrupting or bothering the other students, she would let him do what he wanted. This went on for quite some time. She did not start interacting with him immediately. She allowed time for him to feel safe and calm in the classroom.

Then came what I see as the turning point. Angela had built a level of trust with Isaiah and she could have conversations with him. She would try to gauge him. She got a math journal from a first-grade colleague. But she couldn't give him that journal because the title "First Grade" was printed on it. She made copies of everything because he would not know what level it was. If he had known it was first grade material he would think she was giving him "Baby" work and that would just set him off again. When the class was doing math boxes, she would copy the first-grade math boxes and tell him that she wanted him to do math boxes that he could do without help. Sometimes Angela would have to prove to Isaiah that these were the right boxes for him. He would get out the fourth-grade journal to do the boxes his peers were doing. She would have to remind him that math boxes had to be done independently and she would not be able to help him. She would have to ask him, "Do you want boxes you can't do or are you going sit and do these?" He would eventually get around to doing the ones he was able to do. Occasionally Angela would give him fourth grade boxes that he could do with manipulatives or a number line or a multiplication chart. Most of the time he couldn't do the fourth-grade work. But little by little he started to do some of the academic material his peers were working on. It was because he wanted to. He wanted to be like the other kids. He wanted to be successful. He held out for a long time. Every student wants to be successful but it is up to the teacher to establish a learning environment to enable that to happen. Isaiah did not function or learn like the other twenty-two students in that classroom but he could operate at his level in that classroom because of the teacher.

One of the tools with which many teachers are not familiar is finding a student's Zone of Proximal Development. Angela figured out that Isaiah could perhaps do first grade math. Zone of Proximal Development is approximately, with a little bit of a challenge, the place where students should enter the curriculum and that's where she placed Isaiah. It was a little bit of a challenge but it was manageable. It was the academic level where he could experience success.

Angela wanted to emphasize that she had expectations for Isaiah. During those times when she let him do what he wanted to do he knew that he was not allowed to make noises. He was not allowed to talk to the other students. When she was giving whole group instruction and knew that it wasn't something he needed to be doing because he wasn't ready she also knew that he needed to be doing something academic that was at his Zone of Proximal Development level. He didn't have free reign. He knew what the expectations were for him during those times. Those expectations were not for him to sit in his seat nor to have his eyes on Angela paying full attention to what she was saying. She never expected that of him. It was not important to have him doing that. Making him do that wasn't going to help him to learn anything. By the same token, she didn't need to spend time and energy worrying about managing his behavior when she was trying to instruct the rest of the class. When the paraprofessional did come there were activities the Angela needed him to complete during that time when there was help available. However, he didn't want to leave the room. The paraprofessional would work with him in the back of the room but only for limited periods of time. She too had to learn how to gauge Isaiah's moods. His attention span was very short and what he was able to do was very limited. His work times were very short. But the paraprofessional was in the room for ninety minutes so they would work for 5-10 minutes and then maybe listen to what the rest of the class was doing for a few minutes and then the paraprofessional would reengage him in his tasks. The paraprofessional was a retired special education teacher who had just left the classroom and she had just come back to school to do this job. She was concerned that Angela wanted him to do what the other students were doing and once she realized that was of least concern, she was able to work at his pace. Letter grades were not recorded for Isaiah. His grade card was his progress report from the Special Education Department. There was no point in trying to assign letter grades to him. He was not in an academic place. Academics were the very least of focus areas for Isaiah for the majority of time that he was in Angela's class. It was about getting him to the place where he knew what it looked like and felt like to be a learner, not about what he was learning or if he was growing academically. He needed to know what learning felt like because he had never had that experience. The emotional state that he was in when he arrived in Angela's fourth grade classroom had been caused by his being put in settings with unattainable expectations to look like everyone else. Isaiah had been put in situations to do things that he wasn't capable of doing. He just had to invoke that "Fight or Flight" response. She needed him to trust that every day when he came to school she would not hassle him to do things he was not capable of doing and that took a long time, a very long time. He had been in school for several years and he had never been able to have that kind of trust. He didn't trust anybody.

Because of the work that was accomplished that year with Angela, Isaiah did well in fifth grade. He was actually doing very well toward the end of fourth grade. He started to participate in one of the guided reading groups. For a while he just went to the group to listen. He could sit for twenty minutes and listen to the reading and the discussions. He had a folder like everybody else in the group and he had a book like everybody else and he had assignments like everybody else. Initially, he wouldn't do the work but Angela recognized when she could insist that he do it. In time he started wanting to take a turn during the oral reading times. Everybody was very patient with him and would help him when they could. I think it is imperative at this point that I mention the culture Angela had established in her classroom. The expectation was for students to respect individual differences and it was not acceptable for anyone to criticize or mock other students.

It became apparent after a while that Isaiah knew more than what he had first demonstrated. Somewhere along the line he had picked up more written language than he had been willing to share. He could do some reading and some of the work that other students were doing. He was never expected to take written reading assessments. Angela shared that she never expected that he would be able to do what fourth grade peers were doing but was pleasantly surprised. Once he showed that he wanted to give it a try, she let him try. By the time Isaiah was ready for fifth grade, the teachers had a transition meeting and Angela knew which teacher would be able to work best with him and continue to move his academic progress forward. She visited with this teacher to let her know that it was only recently (last two months of the school year) that they had gotten to the place where she didn't have to constantly be concerned about his behavior. Isaiah was beginning to "go with the flow" and acting like a "student". He had gotten to the point where he couldn't be distinguished from any other student. His behaviors were no different from any other fourth grade student. Angela was able to scaffold Isaiah's academic program. In other words she had met him where he was and slowly built upon prior knowledge until he could perform within the general education classroom at a reasonably similar level.

I know that when I first visited Angela's classroom I would be go around and help students. Initially, Isaiah wanted nothing to do with me. Towards the end of the year he was a little more receptive to assistance. I knew that it was not easy for him to accept help but he was able to do it. He didn't look any different or act any different.

To let a child get to that point of frustration that Isaiah was in when he first came to Angela is unconscionable. He was not a behavior disordered

Charyll Boggs

child but the system he had been in was a contributing factor creating such a personality. You know I liked it when Angela said he learned "how to do school". It seems that once he could do some level of math and some level of reading, he liked how that felt and it is well documented that success breeds success. She set him up for that success.

Why do we make kids like Isaiah struggle to do grade level curriculum? If you can help them grow academically from where they are, isn't that the goal of our profession? Why do we think they all have to look the same? Isaiah's special education teacher was concerned about giving Isaiah letter grades. Why do we worry about grades? If a baby can't crawl, how can we expect them to walk or run? We can't worry about grades when we are working on helping a student get through the day without getting angry or hitting someone or banging their head on the wall. And that was the goal of Isaiah's mother. She wanted him to feel safe and be able to stay in school. The teacher the next year had much higher expectations for Isaiah than Angela but she would say that she remembered him from the previous year and she was thankful for the student he had become. I know that we need high stakes testing but not all students will reach that "proficient level". Nevertheless, they will be successful adults because we can help them learn all they can learn academically and teach them the social skills to be responsible citizens.

I think Angela and Isaiah's story is a clear example of several ideas that I've presented throughout this book. I don't know if she was consciously doing "best teaching practice". She was just doing what was right for Isaiah!! She accepts kids for who they are and where they are and helps them to have the most positive experience possible while in her care.

54

She sets high expectations for her students but they are not the same expectations for every child.

What I believe about the effects of good teachers can be demonstrated by the graph below. It is research conducted by Robert Marzano. (Marzano, Marzano, & Pickering, 2003, p.3) The point of the research is to emphasize the impact that effective teachers have on student achievement versus the effect that less effective schools or less effective teachers have on student achievement. Not only can least effective teachers impede student achievement but they can actually cause students to lose ground in a relatively short time. Conversely, a most effective teacher can assist students to not only keep pace with their academic growth but exceed normal learning expectations.

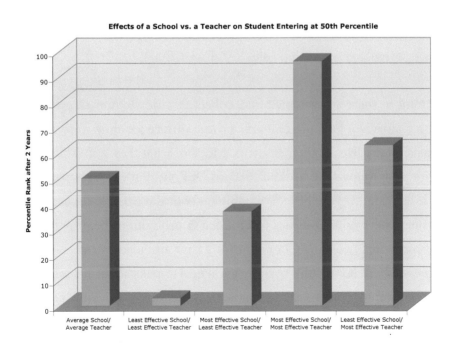

Effects of a School vs. a Teacher on Student Entering at 50th Percentile

In his latest book, Michael Fullan says that "we are stuck with the fact that the quality of teachers is the single most important factor in student learning and that it is uneven at best." (Fullan, 2010, p. 85)

I am proud to say that I see my daughter as one of those "Most Effective Teachers". Currently she is the administrator of a very large elementary school with over 750 students. She has become a teacher leader who supports her peers in working to meet the needs of all students.

> Teaching and leading are clearly distinguishable occupations, but every great leader is clearly teaching and every great teacher is leading. (Gardner, 1989, p.18)

> ...the sense of mission and passion for making a difference that drives highly effective teachers will not find its full expression until they are able to step forward and assume leadership roles. (McEwan, 2002, p. 37)

I want to share an example of the collective efficacy of teacher leaders. It's a story about four teachers and the difference they were able to make in the lives of their students. Much of what they were able to accomplish follows the work of Richard DuFour. But these four teachers probably know very little, if anything, about the work of Richard DuFour. Richard DuFour is a forerunner in promoting the principles of Professional Learning Communities. I have attended two state conferences where he was the keynote speaker. He talks about his tenure as superintendent at Adlai Stevenson High School in Lincolnshire, Illinois. DuFour describes his conversations with teachers about working together to ensure success for all kids. His school was one of the lowest performing schools in Illinois. He attributes much of that incredible improvement that this school experienced during his tenure to the systematic formation of Professional Learning Communities. He has authored 5 books and more than 50 professional articles in recent years around the concept of Professional Learning Communities. What are Professional Learning Communities?

> The very essence of a learning community is a focus on and a commitment to the learning of each student. When a school or district functions as a PLC, educators within the organization embrace high levels of learning for all students as both the reason the organizations exists and the fundamental responsibility of those who work within it. In order to achieve this purpose, the members of a PLC create and are guided by a clear and compelling vision of what the organization must become in order to help all students learn. They make collective commitments clarifying what each member will do to create such an organization, and they use results-oriented goals to mark their progress. Members work together to clarify exactly what each student must learn, monitor each student's learning on a timely basis, provide systematic interventions that ensure students receive additional time and support for learning when they struggle, and extend and enrich learning when students have already mastered the intended outcomes. (DuFour, Dufour, & Eaker, 2006, p. 3)

Now that definition is quite a mouthful. Simply put, effective PLC's are groups of educators working collaboratively to ensure success for all students. Their work is data driven and the teachers understand that success is based on results.

This is a story of dedication to the success of all students. As it is with all states, our state has a process for high stakes testing. Our state has established curricular standards that specific grade levels are responsible for teaching. Secondly, the state has designed assessments based on those standards. The expectation is that all students become proficient or better in their knowledge of the identified standards. Our state assessments are well designed and are a good measuring stick with regard to identifying the level of student proficiency. Something that I find admirable is our state's support for students and teachers. Teachers have the opportunity to access via the internet formative assessments aligned to the state assessments. These formative assessments are for use in classrooms throughout the year. There is always a great deal of discussion around "teaching to the test". I always like to use the example of requiring students to know states and capitals. If a teacher expects her students to pass a test on states and capitals, would she not teach states and capitals and would students not be expected to practice those states and capitals?

This group of four teachers, this learning community if you will, included two first-year teachers, one teacher with six years of experience and the teacher leader in this group had fourteen years of experience and was a life-long learner. These teachers started using the formative assessments and looking at the data. Here is the powerful part of this process. They began to involve their students when examining the results of the formative assessments. They would talk about what they did well and areas where they needed to do some work. The students kept data folders with their goals and running records of progress, areas where they needed more work and areas where they were doing well. This process of setting and tracking personal goals is a powerful and effective way to help students "own" their learning. Sometimes we expect students to be successful with their having little or no knowledge of end goal. When they have clearly articulated goals and are able to meet those goals, we see that excitement for learning and find again that success breeds success.

> Highly effective teachers know that it is only when students are empowered to take charge of their own learning that a teacher's true mission has been accomplished. Meihenbaum and Biemiller call it nurturing independent learners. They describe a process of student goal setting that makes students "much more likely to engage in deliberate practice, to intentionally plan and self-monitor their performance, and to persist in the face of failure and frustration." Teacher-leaders nurture goal setting and help students understand how the achievement of a goal will bring added value to their lives (e.g., once you learn to read on your own, you won't have to wait for someone to read aloud to you or once you are able to write well, you won't have to worry about completing essays for job or college applications). Teacher-leaders ask students to reflect on their learning by regularly asking them to write responses to questions like these (a) When can you use what you learned today? (b). What did you like best (or least) about today's class? (c). What do you know you know? (Meichenbaum & Biemiller, 1998; McEwan, 2002, p. 40)

In the meantime, the teachers continued to meet, on their own time because there was no scheduled collaboration time. They continued to brainstorm strategies for helping their students to become proficient in the knowledge of grade level standards.

This process continued for about six months. Periodically the students would take another formative assessment and examine where they were getting stronger and where they still needed to focus their attention. The important part of this process is that teachers are expected to teach the standards set by the state and they have the information that lets them know what students know and what still needs to be taught.

Back to the story. The students in these four classrooms started to get excited each time they took another formative assessment. They wanted to know how they'd done, had they done better, what areas need additional work? Students began to OWN the learning. They now understood what they needed to do, they understood what they were responsible for, and they understood where they were in their learning and how they were moving along. They began to set goals for themselves. When it came time for the state assessment the teachers believed the students were academically prepared to take the assessments and they turned their focus to setting a climate in the classroom that encourages students to want to work as a team and give all they were able to give to help the class as a whole demonstrate their learning. The staff organized a Pep Rally around the concept of "winning the game of state assessments". The students made up cheers to perform in front the of the student body. The teachers put together skits and songs to reinforce test taking strategies. The high school drum core even came to set the rally in motion. Kids were so excited and so engaged. It was heartwarming to witness such a sense of community and a feeling that "we're all in this together and together we will succeed". As might be expected, they not only succeeded but surpassed expectation. They were later recognized and honored on a national level for achieving success with ALL the students. The school community for these four teachers is not affluent, is not without a diverse population but staff would always strive to make sure that they taught what ALL students needed to learn to be successful.

This school has evolved, due in large part to the work of this collaborative group of teachers. There are schools, teachers if you will, who only teach the tested indicators for the state assessments. As this staff has evolved, they have come to understand that the tested indicators must be taught but must be taught in an authentic, organized manner and within the appropriate curriculum at the appropriate time. For instance, students do "math boxes" once a week. These boxes have problems that would review state indicators, teachers go over them with students and talk about them. Then at a later date those indicators are reviewed to see if students truly "own" that information. Teachers don't try to force it into students' memories through memorization or "drill and kill". Indicators are taught at an appropriate time as it fits into the curriculum and reviewed at regular intervals until it becomes part of what kids know and are able to do.

Questions to ponder:
- What are your thoughts and revelations about Angela and Isaiah's situation?
- Should teachers be teaching standards instead of letting textbooks drive their instruction?
- When teaching the standards, if there is evidence that students have mastered particular standards, what is the next step?
- Is teaching standards a process familiar to most teachers? Why? Why not?
- Are you a member of a functioning PLC?
- What is the RIGHT thing to do for our students?

Chapter 5

Real Schools

My story continues as I take the position of administrator at a pre-K through sixth grade elementary school. This school was about four times larger than my previous school and was in an extremely affluent community. But as I was to discover, children are basically the same regardless of who the parents are or where they live. And parents are basically the same in that they all do the best they can for their children and they expect us to meet the needs of their children at whatever level might be necessary. And indeed, that should be our challenge as educators – to meet the needs of each and every child because they are somebody's child.

One thought that stands out as memorable at this school of 600 students is the importance of being able to call a student by name. Now, remembering names is not a strength for me but it became abundantly clear one day when I called a student by name and he said, "Do you know everybody's name?" I just replied, "I try to know them." That's when it became so apparent that knowing students' names was important to the students. I had to put more emphasis on forming a personal relationship with each of my 600 students. One of the ways I addressed this goal was by giving each student a book on his/her birthday. I bought a chest for large picture books that were meant for kindergarten and first grade students and another bookshelf for chapter books purchased with older students in mind. The chest and bookshelf were housed in the front office. My media specialist kept the chest and bookshelf filled with books that she knew students would most enjoy. Students would come into the office on their birthday and select a book of their choice. They would bring the book to me and I would sign it with a birthday greeting personally addressed to them. This provided me with an opportunity to have a personal connection with each child every year. I believe that it's not just teachers that impact students' development and learning but all adults that touch that child's life. This includes coaches, sponsors, Sunday School teachers, grandparents, and all those in the extended family and even the school leader.

"Locate a resilient kid and you will also find a caring adult
– or several – who guided him." (Payne, 2013, p. 101).

There was another experience I had when I began to work in this new environment. It was, without a doubt, another learning experience for me. After several months of observation, I found that the standard procedure for the K-2nd grade staff was to teach whole group reading instruction using a basal, regardless of students' instructional (readiness) level. There was support for students who had been identified as Special Education students receiving services from the special education staff. It became apparent that the students who were at a more developed level of performance were not being challenged during the literacy block. I assembled the K-2nd grade staff and we began to hold discussions around strategies for meeting the needs of ALL students. My belief is that all students need instruction within their zone of proximal development. At the early elementary level this does not translate into the same instruction for all students nor the same instructional materials. These teachers were using the same story out the basal for all students. Throughout the week these students were reading the same story either in pairs or aloud with the teacher or individually. I met with these teachers on a weekly basis. I planned staff development around appropriate reading strategies including differentiated instruction. We attended conferences and teachers led staff development days around the topic of Differentiated Instruction. This was our focus for two years. Differentiated Instruction is a strategy that allows students to pursue different avenues to learning content. It allows for students to process, construct or make sense of the content and teachers to develop materials so that all students can learn effectively regardless of differences in abilities.

> Differentiated instruction, according to Carol Ann Tomlinson, is the process of "ensuring that what a student learns, how he/she learns it, and how the student demonstrates what he/she has learned is a match for that student's readiness level, interests, and preferred mode of learning. (Ellis, Gable, Greg, & Rock, 2008, p. 32),

We had guest lecturers to train the staff in how to conduct guided reading groups. We also investigated the strategies that support a Balanced Literacy Program. When writing our school improvement plan we identified Balanced Literacy as our reading program. For the remainder of that first school year I, personally, met with the higher performing students for thirty minutes at the end of the day in an effort to provide enriched instruction and activities. While these young students were very adept at reading they were not familiar with the writing process. We started working on higher level writing skills connected to their basal story. I presented higher level thinking/writing challenges. That was my initial strategy for modeling appropriate instruction based on student readiness and need. To prepare for the following year my local parent organization provided funding to purchase leveled reading materials. I believed that once I had secured the materials and provided training around effective reading instruction we would be ready to move forward. My next step was to build a learning community. It should be obvious by now that I totally support professional learning communities. I find that, done well, PLC's provide improved learning opportunities for students. As I approached the format to establish PLC's, I experienced quite a bit of passive resistance. I thought perhaps a black and white approach might be the best approach to this resistance. I arranged, through the use of substitute teachers, for my classroom teachers and the special education staff to have time each week to meet and discuss topics related to Balanced Literacy and differentiated instruction. As we moved into the next school year I asked each primary teacher to complete a running record for every student in their classroom. A running record is a quick assessment where students read an unfamiliar passage and the teacher tracks numbers of words and reading errors. Depending on the student's performance, the teacher can identify the student's reading level. Each teacher was provided a different color set of index cards (i.e. blue cards, yellow cards, green cards, pink cards, etc.). They were to record their students' scores and current reading levels on their index cards. All twelve teachers brought their index cards to our collaborative meeting. I had them group all the students (about 240 students) according to reading levels (level A, level B, level C and so on). They could readily see that within one group there were blue cards, yellow cards, green cards, etc. We discussed how we might better utilize our instructional time and resources, including special education staff, if we put students in the appropriate guided reading group at the appropriate instructional level. This would reduce the number of small groups that each teacher would need to meet with on a regular basis and allow for more focused instruction at students' instructional levels. These guided reading groups would not be the entire reading program as Balanced Literacy included shared reading, guided reading, read alouds and independent reading, which they professed could be done with their homeroom groups. We tried this guided reading process, sharing students, for the entire school year. We kept the groups flexible so students could move between leveled groups when regular monitoring dictated. The beginning of the next year we met to discuss our plans for the upcoming year and those passive frustrations were expressed aloud. As I sat wondering where this process was failing, one of the teachers said, "I think the problem is we just don't trust. We don't trust that when any of our students go to another teacher for guided reading instruction they are getting what they would be getting with me." Oh, My Gosh!! After two years of intensive work collaboratively, decreasing the amount of planning because teachers could plan for two or three as opposed to five or six reading groups, and a plethora of new materials, they didn't "Trust" one another. They wanted to revert to teaching all of their own assigned students. They were willing to work to address diverse instructional levels of students, continue working on a Balanced Literacy Program and use leveled reading materials but they were not comfortable sharing students. What did this say to me? Where had I failed the teachers and the students?

> Without trust, the best we can do is compromise; without trust, we lack the credibility for open, mutual learning and communication and real creativity. (Covey, 1990, p. 220)

> When the Consortium on Chicago School Research compared the 30 most highly rated schools in Chicago with 30 of the lowest performing ones, it discovered the questions related to the quality of relationships – in particular, the level of trust and respect teachers have for one another – were among the best predictors of school performance. (McREL, 2009, Vol. 60)

This concept of trust between my teachers or even trust between myself and the teachers reminded me of the experience that I had in the transformation of my little K-8 from a traditional school setting to a modern age, multi-age format. Both were huge turning points for me with regards to my belief system. Because I was being challenged on a daily basis, I had to know in my heart that what I was doing was doing what was "right for kids" because it could cost me my job and my reputation as an educator. I was quickly convinced by the results we were getting on test scores, in student behaviors and from other educators around the state that it was "right".

> Resolving fears and anxiety created by change is a major task for those leading school improvement. Taking time

to ensure that the reasons for the change, the practicality of this program for the specific problem being addressed, and the philosophical basis for the effort are well understood by everyone involved will enhance the likelihood of lasting implementation. (SEDL.org, 2009, pg. 7)

Eventually I began working as an educational consultant for an education service center. The purpose of that center is to provide service and assistance to school districts across the state as they work to meet federal and state mandates and educate the youth of their community. I found myself, regardless of the material or topic I had been assigned or requested to address, delivering the same message. That message was and continues to be grounded in my basic belief system about children and about our role as educators. My belief can be very simply stated and that is that EVERY KID COUNTS. However, the message I delivered to every group with whom I worked was grounded in establishing relationships with students. What does that mean "relationships with students"? It means that if students do not feel an authentic connection to the adults with whom they have contact, they will not feel any obligation to respond to the expectations of those adults. One would think this concept would be a matter of common sense. As sensible as this may appear, it is a practice consistently ignored or shunned by a huge number of educators. I refer back to Stephen Covey's "deposits" and "withdrawals" that educators, in fact many adults, make to their relationships with students. Some of these transactions are intentionally practiced, but frequently adults are unintentionally using a practice that establishes a less than positive relationship. As I considered this project of telling my story, sharing my thoughts and beliefs, I have referred to some well-known and respected experts in the field of education. As I read their work, it was almost without exception that I found they all referred to the critical role that teacher-student relationships played in the success of all kids. I would like to share a few of the quotes that I found from our esteemed colleagues.

> No significant learning occurs without a significant relationship. Dr. James Comer stated simply: positive relationships are essential to a child's ability to grow up healthy and achieve later social, emotional, and academic success. Those "positive relationships" begin with the adults in the school building and district. The personal rapport among teachers, students, and parents influences students' school attendance and their sustained efforts at difficult school tasks. (Blankstein, 2004, p. 59)

That is not always easy. Some students don't consciously open that door to let adults into their lives. In fact, some work diligently to keep that door locked. I have witnessed over the last forty years the struggle that educators face on a daily basis. Some things I've learned from years of teaching and some from parenting. I have a fairly poignant example of how some teachers might view the idea of "relationship with students". When I work with high school teachers I try to emphasize the importance of making a connection with students. One does not need to expend the time and effort to form a strong relationship with every student because some students don't need or want that relationship. I have a very independent and self-driven granddaughter. A teacher need only present the expectations of the class and leave her alone to complete the necessary tasks. However, if the teacher does not try to form some type of relationship with my grandson, their time with him will be less than enjoyable and he, to his own detriment, will be less than successful. He is a very personable and approachable young man. He can easily connect with any young or old person, male or female. However, if that person has no interest in connecting with him, he's done with them. This includes teachers. He needs that adult to form a connection with him, talk to him, listen to him, get to know what motivates him.

Let me share a less than positive example of forming a good working relationship with students. As I was working with one high school staff, they shared that there was a young man with whom many teachers had worked and seemed less than successful. They shared that this young man kept getting detentions for his misbehavior. I inquired as to what that detention might look like. It was shared that he would have eat his lunch in an isolated setting away from his peers. I then asked how many of those type of detentions this young man had to serve. It was shared that he had 220 (there were only 102 days of school left in the academic school year). As one might guess, I asked if they thought their consequences for this young man's behavior were of any consequence to him? They truly had no reasonable explanation for what was happening. It didn't appear that any time had been spent trying to problem solve this situation. If some level of problem solving had taken place I don't believe that the young man would have had more detentions than there were days of school left. It is somewhat sad to see all students receiving the same consequence for misbehaviors especially when it becomes evident that the consequence clearly is not modifying the misbehavior at all.

The most effective schools provide a ladder of opportunities for struggling students, ranging from identification of students needing extra support before the school year begins to mandatory enrollment in remedial and/or skills classes. The effect of this range of interventions is to make clear to students that they may *not* fail. It tells students that the only choice is to learn and succeed. An effective improvement plan for all students includes components of both prevention and intervention. Some prevention strategies are targeted; others apply to the entire student population. The latter include:

- Building relationships with students
- Systematically identifying and building on students' strengths
- Meeting with students each day
- Having staff be visible and available
- Involving students in the decision-making process. (Blankstein, 2002, p. 111-112)

When I read *Failure is Not an Option* by Alan M. Blankstein I thought about the many children that have in the past and are currently struggling to find success in school. How can we believe that is acceptable? I had a disheartening experience while doing some consulting work with a middle school staff. The day was organized so that I would first work with the sixth-grade teachers, then the seventh and then the eighth. With each group I opened the session with a bit of inquiry about the culture of their school. My question was, "Is failure an option in your school?" And the answer was, without exception, "Not for kids who want to do well." But they said there were kids that didn't want to be successful. And I asked if they truly believed that. Did they truly believe that kids wanted to fail? We discussed that thought for quite a while and they shared experiences of kids failing and expressing a lack of caring. At one point, one teacher said, "I don't want you to tell me it's my fault." Why would she think I would say that? Perhaps because as the conversation moved on it became clear that there was a culture in the school that accepted the false reality that kids would consciously choose to fail. The staff shared the story of a young man who had multiple detentions and was failing most of his classes. One of those classes was a social studies class that was structured in the following manner. The teacher lectured on a daily basis and gave a ten-point quiz at the end of class. This young man had just that day received a score of 4 on the ten-point quiz and announced, "Maybe tomorrow I'll get a 3". I asked that teacher if he thought the young man truly intended to fail and he responded, "That's what he said". In my mind I was silently thinking, "Wow! This is not a culture that is supportive of success for all students." But I decided to offer some suggestions to support this teacher and this student. I asked if there were a possibility of this young man receiving some "pre-teaching" of the material and the group didn't see where that was a possibility. When I approached the concept of spending time with this student outside the regularly scheduled class time, I was told that it would just take too much time. (I always try to impress upon a teacher when they give me that excuse, that it truly is time well invested and will save time down the road dealing with misbehaviors.) I next suggested that there were probably some essential concepts that this teacher wanted all students to know from his class. I asked if it would be possible for this young man to be given three or four questions around those essential learning concepts before the lecture. This would provide a guide for this student and he would know what he was listening for during the lecture time. The teacher that taught this class said that could be a possibility but also suggested that the other students might want the same thing. In my thinking I didn't see anything wrong with giving all students a guide to the lesson or a graphic organizer for them with prompts so they would know what it was they were to remember. I felt like the conversation took a positive turn at that point. Again, it sometimes comes down to teachers not possessing the tools with which to address issues that they face on a daily basis. In my opinion, if students are truly not demonstrating that they have learned the information the teacher intended for them to learn then it should be the teacher's responsibility to find another way to deliver that information.

It was the culture of this staff which most piqued my interest.

> An examination of school culture is important because, as Goodlad's study (1984) points out, alike as schools may be in many ways, each school has an ambience (or culture) of its own and, further, its ambience may suggest to the careful observer useful approaches to making it a better school. Krueger and Parish in their study of five districts implementing and then discontinuing programs, postulate that the key to program implementation and continuation is the interactive relationships that teachers have worked out together regarding "how we get things done here". Depending upon how well leaders understand and use this notion, culture can assist school improvement efforts for at-risk students, or act as a barrier to change. (SEDL, (1992) pg. 1)

It bears repeating from this article by SEDL, culture can assist school improvement efforts for at-risk students or act as a barrier to change.

Every school has a culture, a way of "doing business". I have had the opportunity to see this fact in action over the years. A "way of doing business" refers to how we interact with students, parents and colleagues. It is the way we address or perhaps don't address issues on a daily basis. If we have a culture of believing that some students don't want to succeed then we tend to ensure that belief by *not* instilling a practice of doing whatever is necessary to make sure that all students do indeed succeed to high standards. We, in fact, build the barrier to success.

> The term **school culture** generally refers to the beliefs, perceptions, relationships, attitudes, and written and unwritten rules that shape and influence every aspect of how a school functions, but the term also encompasses more concrete issues such as the physical and emotional safety of students, the orderliness of classrooms and public spaces, or the degree to which a school embraces and celebrates racial, ethnic, linguistic, or cultural diversity. Generally speaking, school cultures can be divided into two basic forms: positive cultures and negative cultures. Broadly defined positive school cultures are conducive to professional satisfaction, morals, and effectiveness, as well as to student learning, fulfillment, and well-being. (Education Glossary, 2014).

Society expects better results than they have been receiving over the past several decades. If different results are the expectation that we must equip teachers with different tools because they are using all the tools they currently have at their disposal. What does the term "different tools" look like? I believe teachers are intelligent, creative and hard-working people. Collectively they can solve almost any problem by working together and utilizing their individual strengths and skills. Unfortunately, classroom teachers are rarely provided the training or time to capitalize on such well researched strategies as professional learning communities or data-driven instruction. Why is that the case? School districts across our state and across our country continue to face bigger and more challenging issues. They are expected to meet the highest of expectations through high stakes testing and mandates that outline quality and performance indicators for improvement. Perhaps the best-known model of teacher training was developed by Bruce R. Joyce and Beverly Showers. Together they outline the components of results-based staff development as the most effective manner in which to train teachers, ultimately resulting in improved student achievement. The research shows that if new concepts are just presented to staff during a lecture or workshop, the impact for application in the classroom results in about 10% impact. However, if the new concepts are presented, modeled, practiced with low risk feedback and coaching with peers, specialists, or administration, the impact for application in the classroom results in about 95% impact.

Researchers Joyce and Showers argue that professional development (PD) is often based on the belief that once teachers learn and develop a skill, they will automatically use it in the classroom. They found that learned knowledge and skills are rarely, if ever, transferred to the classroom.

The authors identify four key components of training. The first focuses on *knowledge* and consists of exploring the *theory* or rationale for the new skills or strategies.

A Passion for the Teaching and Learning Process

Subsequently, they suggest, training needs to involve *modelling* the new skills – ideally in a setting closely approximate to the workplace. The third component is the *practice* of the skill and the authors estimate a substantial period of time (8–10 weeks, involving around 25 trials) to "bring a teaching model of medium complexity under control". Finally, *peer coaching*, the fourth component, is the collaborative work of teachers in planning and developing the lessons and materials to implement the training effectively. (Joyce & Showers, 2003).

I want to share one example of a result-based staff development that I used with my staff.

The middle school math and science teachers had participated in an out-of-district staff development activities that addressed problem-solving strategies (awareness). Using release time, these teachers identified the four-step problem-solving model as defined in the scoring rubric for the Kansas state assessments (skill development). During a district staff development day, these same teachers conducted in-service activities that addressed this strategy. The activities progressed from an explanation of the state and district curricular standards to the four-step problem-solving model. Eventually the group worked together to design lessons that could be used in the classroom. The staff was then given the task of reporting back to the group in two weeks at a regular staff meeting and sharing an activity that had been done in their individual classroom that utilized this strategy. Teachers were encouraged to invite a peer to observe their lesson and offer feedback (low-risk practice with feedback). The next step was the process of making signs that were to be displayed in every classroom promoting the use of the four-step problem-solving model (institutionalization).

There is a great deal of time invested with results-based staff development. Because of the time factor it is imperative that schools examine their data and focus on one critical area of instruction at a time. It is one of the ways to improve teacher effectiveness which translates into improved student achievement. Is that not the total intention of the teaching and learning process?

As I referenced earlier I worked as a consultant, a School Improvement Specialist, at an education service center. I also worked for the state as an Implementation Coach. I assisted schools that had been identified as being "On Improvement" and coached the staff through the process of writing a school improvement plan and implementing that plan. It was an eye-opening experience when I first took on the role of consultant traveling around the state to work with a variety of school districts. There were very small districts with a total student population of 200 students and large districts with a student population of 6000. During my consulting work, I worked primarily with the teachers. Sometimes it was the entire staff and sometimes leadership teams. Sometimes district or building administration were involved but all too frequently there were no administrators present during my time with teachers. I find that the administration often does not recognize the impact of their presence and the difference it can make for achieving substantive change within the district. Often teachers are willing to initiate change but feel powerless to do so. They would proceed with initiatives only if they saw that administration was "on board" with those initiatives.

Leaders establish personal credibility far more readily by what they do than by what they say. Expressions of commitment to strong moral purpose only generate cynicism if the commitment is not manifested through behavior. If leaders are to be believed they must establish their personal integrity and 'integrity requires action....' Authentic leaders embody character in action: they don't just say, they do". (DuFour, Dufour, Eaker, Many, 2006, p.194).

I am going to share two very real examples of the difference it can make when the entire school community is involved in the change process. It truly is a matter of collective responsibility, all parties owning the process for systemic change: teachers, administrators, support staff, parents and businesses.

Collective efficacy means that people have confidence in each other. Principals trust, value and depend on their peers. School leaders and district leaders similarly believe in each other's capacity, individually and jointly, to solve problems and make progress. Collective capacity is more than the sum total of individual capacities. It is a powerhouse because it compounds individual efficacy into collective capacity and impact. (Fullan, 2010, p. 45)

Our state is currently providing training in MTSS (Multi-tier Support Systems) or the Ci3T Model of Intervention. It is very similar to the RtI (Response to Intervention) that is included in the existing ESEA Legislation (Elementary and Secondary Education Act). My service center has state trainers who provide this training to schools in whatever format the district prefers. This may be in the form of training every teacher or working with leadership teams and supporting them as they work with their individual staffs. The cornerstones of the MTSS Process include many of the concepts I've discussed in this book. Those include professional development, leadership, empowering cultures and fidelity to curriculum and instruction. At the heart of this process is designing a system that is intended to ensure the success of all students. It is about the prevention of failure and building a system that provides a rapid response with research-based interventions for students who exhibit potential for failure. It was an easy training for me to deliver because it supports what I believe about the institution of education.

I worked with one district that sent two different sets of leadership teams to our MTSS training. Included, however, were the building administrators and the Assistant Superintendent. One of the major changes they were able to make was in how and when language classes were taught in the middle and high schools, based on student need. Students could still receive all of their credits but not all students took the same English classes. Some took classes which provided direct instruction in reading and not classes that focused on grammar. Teachers saw immediate results on their students' state assessment reading scores. Their excitement when they reported back to our training group was so emotional. They have continued to move forward with their efforts at a rapid pace. I recognize that it was not just because the administration supported the teachers' efforts but it was because all stakeholders were working toward the same end which was success for all students.

Here is another story that is not quite as positive. In fact I found it a rather sad tale. For a year these four teachers from a small school were coming to our MTSS training. About mid-year the different schools were sharing their successes and frustrations. This small group felt nothing but frustration. As one of my colleagues and I visited with this group on a one-to-one basis we found that they had great ideas and had worked on a plan for the school but had absolutely no administrative support. Consequently, the rest of their staff was less than willing to participate in the plan that required a change in how they delivered services to students. We offered strategies for ways to accomplish their goals. We suggested that they continue with their planning and go to their administrator with the goal of meeting the needs of all the students in their school. They would need data about the current levels at which their students were performing, where they wanted to be and a plan for getting there. We told them that they may not receive immediate support but this plan stood a better chance of helping to make a change than just giving up and continuing the way they had always "done school".

There is another area which I supported and tried to model – follow-up. Teachers cannot hear about a teaching strategy once and expect to fully and successfully implement it. Whether it is a system change or a change in teaching strategies, it requires focus, follow-up and feedback. This is time-consuming but critical if we truly want to ensure improvement in our teaching and learning process.

Chapter 6

Conclusion

How do I put into words how genuine and passionate I am about attending to the needs of every child? It is our professional, ethical, and moral responsibility to do that and that anyone would have the ability to do that is a gift, a divine gift to have the ability and desire to impact young lives. I can't think of a more important, more rewarding or more difficult job. And I know that my expectations are probably unrealistic but if we don't reach for the moon, if we don't try with every ounce of courage then we will certainly fail many children. If we are going to fail children, we shouldn't be teachers because as Blankstein says "Failure is Not an Option". It is not an option when we're talking about children born of innocence and knowing that the adults in that child's world are responsible for raising and nurturing him/her. There is a familiar African proverb that says, "It takes a whole village to raise a child". We know that some people in the village do not recognize that and don't accept that responsibility. But that is no excuse for us as educators. We chose to become educators. People who become educators make a conscious choice to become teachers and if you are going to chose to be a teacher then you have to have chosen to educate ALL children. That is our job. We have to find the tools, the strength, and the support we need to do whatever we must in an effort to be successful in our chosen profession. If you have children, grandchildren, nieces, nephews, brothers or sisters in an educational setting, isn't that how you want the people who work with those children to think, to feel and to believe. So must we. As educators we must also believe and think in that way.

I know I am over zealous and I know it may seem that I don't truly understand or recognize the day-to-day challenges. But I have seen and worked with educators that make a difference. And they make that difference by looking for ways to accomplish it. They don't wait for those "ways" to come to them, they don't wait for the "silver bullet" that would ensure success for all kids. And they don't use excuses because there is no viable excuse for not meeting the needs of every child, at least no excuse for not truly attempting to make a difference for each child in their charge. If we start doing that with our students, start working on it when they are young and start establishing a school culture that is focused on success for every student we'll stop losing students through that black hole of illiteracy, low self esteem and failure.

I've known a lot of really expert, what we might call, Master Teachers. I believe they are masters at the art of teaching. We are going to have to face reality about the need for helping every child meet with success and grow into a responsible citizen. If we don't our society becomes less educated, less responsible, and ill equipped to deal with the future. We know there are those kids who practically educate themselves. They come from families with strong beliefs in school, in education in general. However, there are many, many kids that have not grown up with those beliefs and we can't let our society become degraded because some of the children with whom we work are more challenging. Little by little I have seen some positive initiatives, including Response to Intervention (RtI), development of Professional Learning Communities (PLC's), and results-based staff development taking form in a large number of school districts. Again, there are pockets of excellence that I've referenced throughout this book. I am always encouraged when I happen upon such a pocket. What defines these pockets of excellence are the outstanding, caring teachers with building and district support. It's not programs, it's not money, it's not functional or dysfunctional families. It's about the teachers who don't allow excuses for not helping kids. The efforts of skilled, dedicated, caring teachers can move mountains. And when I have the opportunity to observe that, my heart is filled with pride and hope for the future.

Bibliography

Anderson, R. H. & Pavan, B. N. (1993). *Non-gradedness: helping it to happen.* Lancaster, PA: Technomic Publishing Co.

Blankstein, A. M. (2004). *Failure is not an option.* Thousand Oaks, CA: Corwin Press. Hope Foundation.

Bpslearningsessions. (2004). *Teacher expectations and student achievement program.* www.bpslearningsessionsweekly.com.

Covey, S. R. (1989). *The 7 habits of highly effective people.* New York, NY: Simon & Schuster.

DuFour, R., Dufour, R., Eaker, R. & Many, T. (2006). *Learning by doing.* Bloomington, IN: Solution Tree.

Fullan, M. (2010). *All systems go.* Thousand Oaks, CA: Corwin: Ontario Principals' Council.

Glossary of Education Reform. (2014). Portland, ME: Great Schools Partnership.

Joyce, B. & Showers, B. (2003). *Student achievement through staff development.* Toronto, Ontario: National College for School Leadership.

Live Science. (2010, August). *Personality set for life by 1st grade, study suggests.* New York, NY.

McEwan, E. K. (2002). *10 Traits of highly effective teachers*. Thousand Oaks, CA: Corwin Press, Inc.

Marzano, R. J. & Pickering, D. J. (2003). *Classroom management that works*. Alexandrea, VA: ASCD.

Marzano, R. J. (2003). *What works in schools*. Alexandria, VA: ASCD.

Meichenbaum, D. & Biemiller, A. (1998). *Nurturing independent learners: helping students take charge of their learning*. Cambridge, MA: Brookline Books.

Mullen, G. (2020). *Maslow before bloom*. www.exploringthecore.com.

NAEYC. (2009). *Developmentally appropriate practice in early childhood programs serving*
children from birth to age 8. Washington, DC: NAEYC.org.

Oliver, B. (2017). *The knowing-doing gap* (Vol. XIV). Alexandria, VA; Just Ask Publications.

Payne, R. (2013). *A framework for understanding poverty*. Highlands, TX: aha! Process, Inc.

Pfeffer, J. & Sutton, R. (2000). *The knowing-doing gap: how smart companies turn knowledge into action*. Boston, MA: Harvard Business School Press.

SEDL. (1992). *School context: bridge or barrier to change*. Austin, TX: Southwest Educational Development Laboratory.

CPSIA information can be obtained
at www.ICGtesting.com
Printed in the USA
BVHW022132010322
630318BV00001B/3

9 781638 674085